Life Under the Sea Coloring Book

Hi everyone,

Thank you so much for purchasing this coloring book. I hope you enjoy it!

I have a special surprise for you…

Claim your gift here: https://bit.ly/2K58AtH

Thanks so much and happy coloring!

Color Test Page

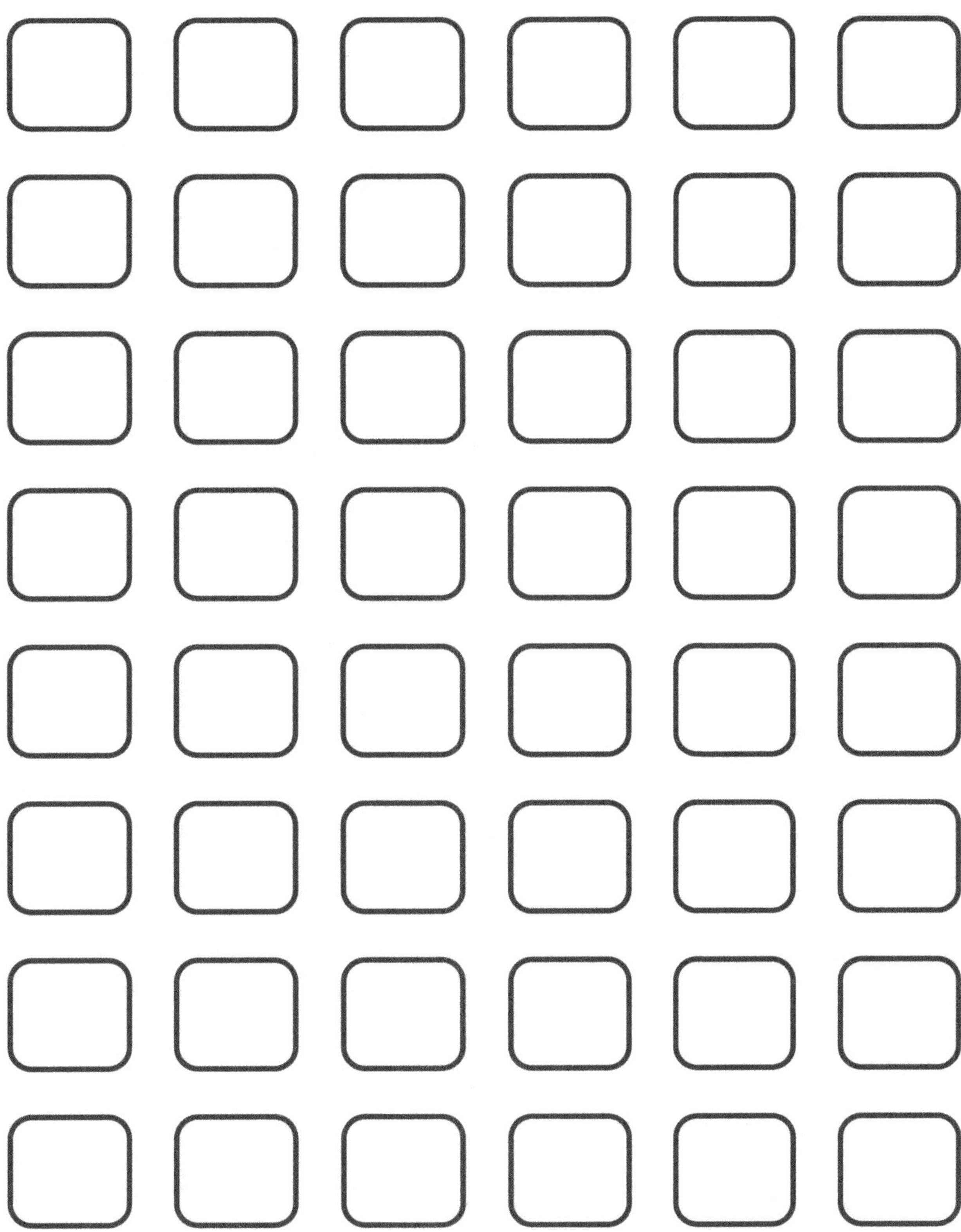

Color Test Page

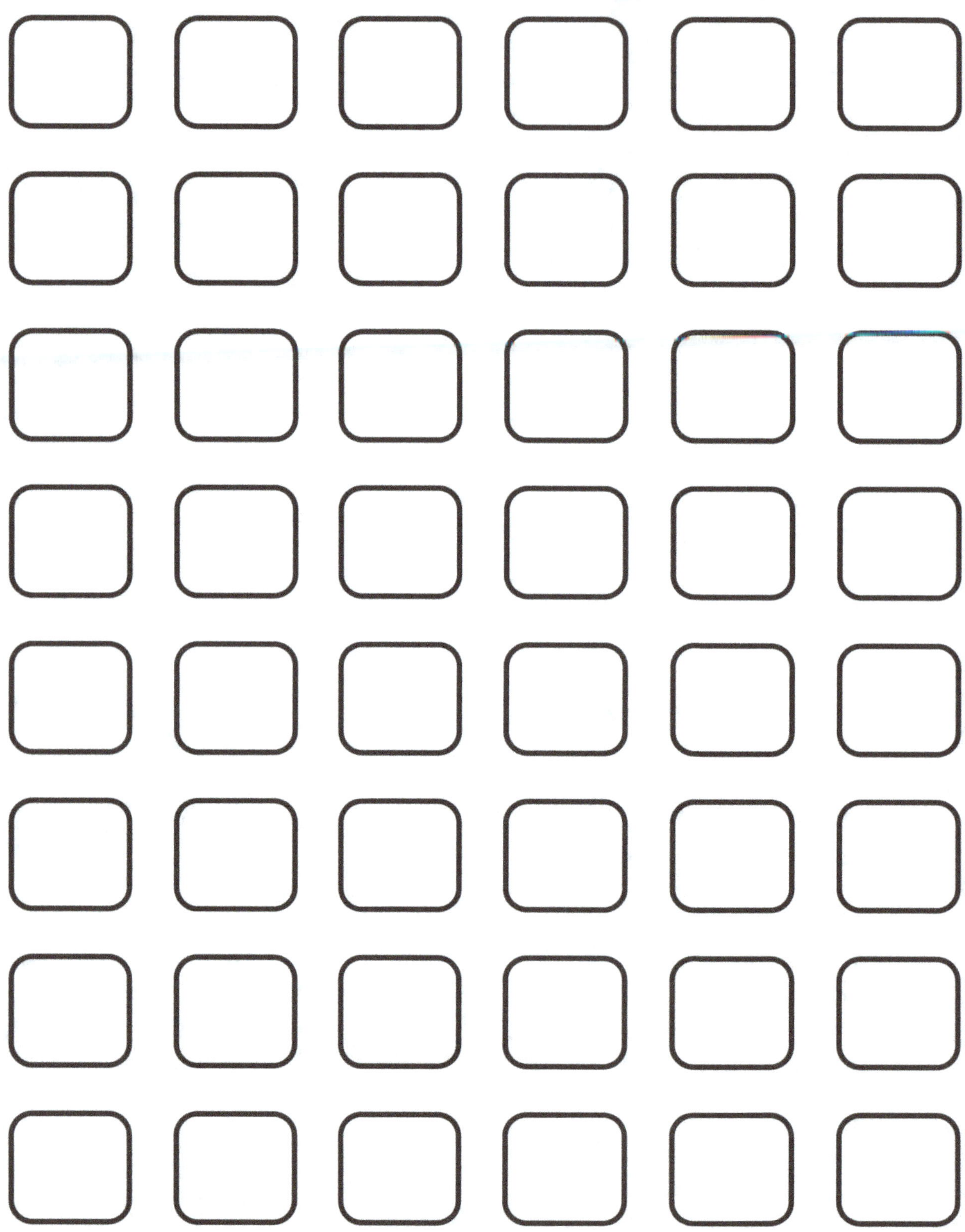

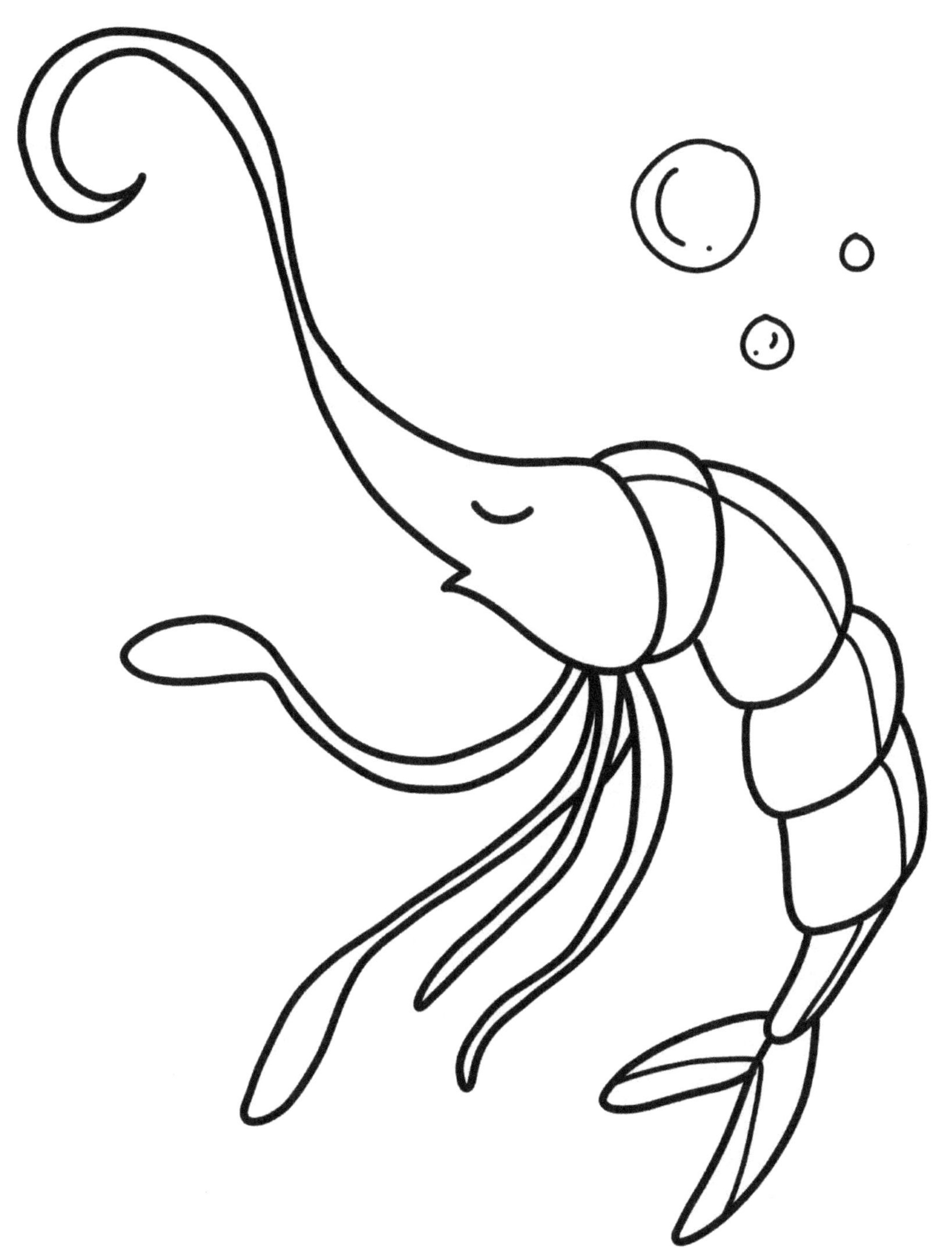

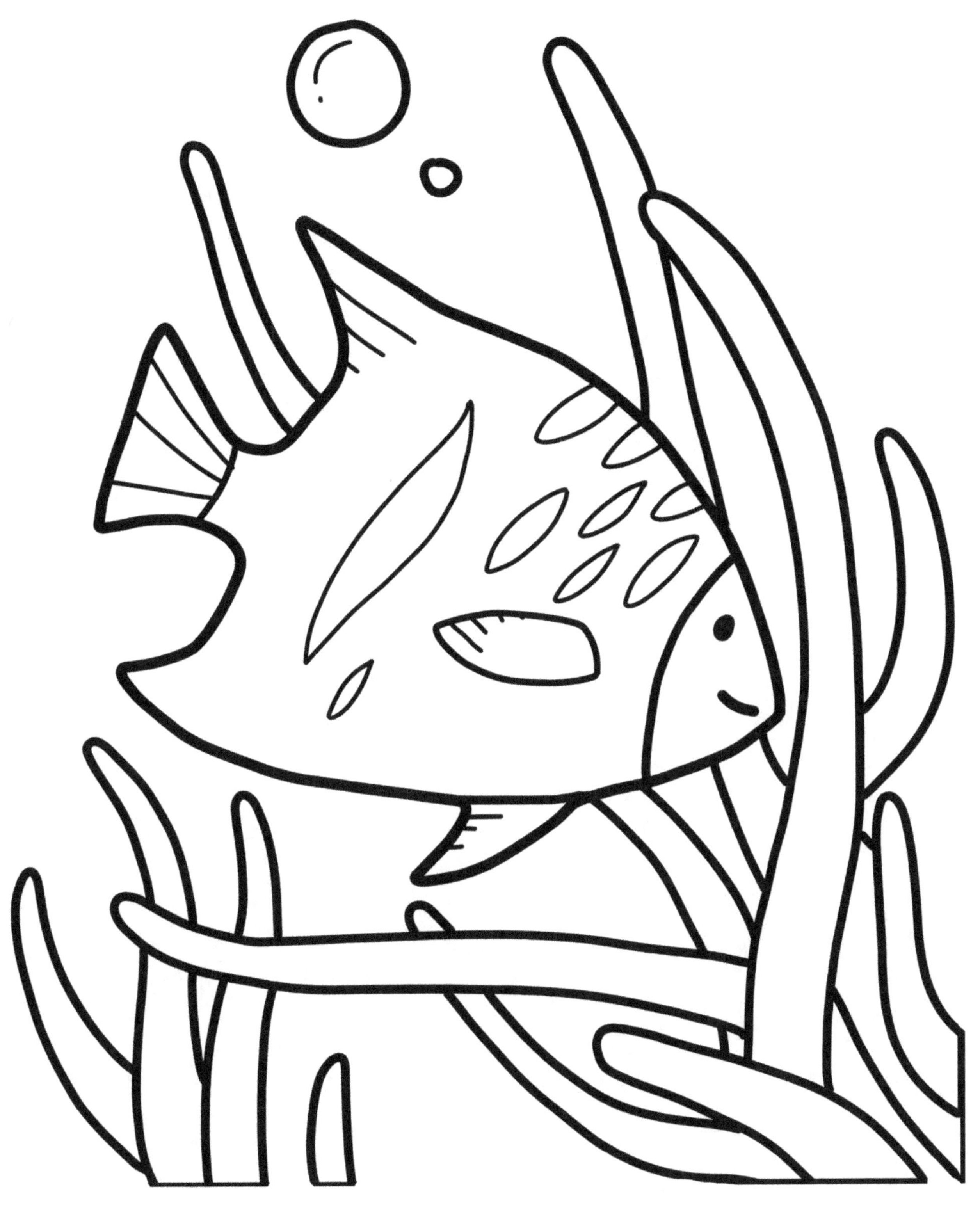

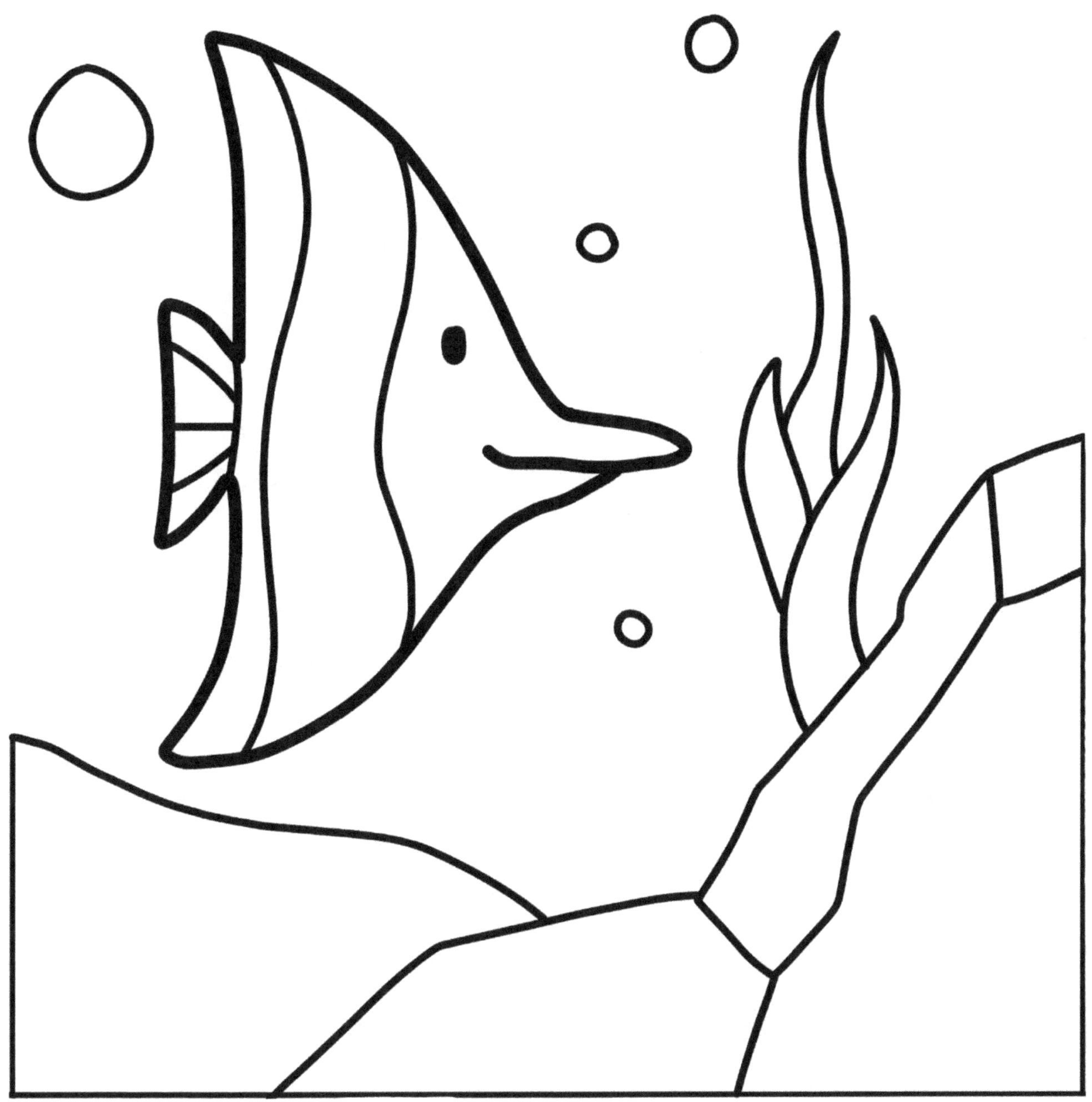

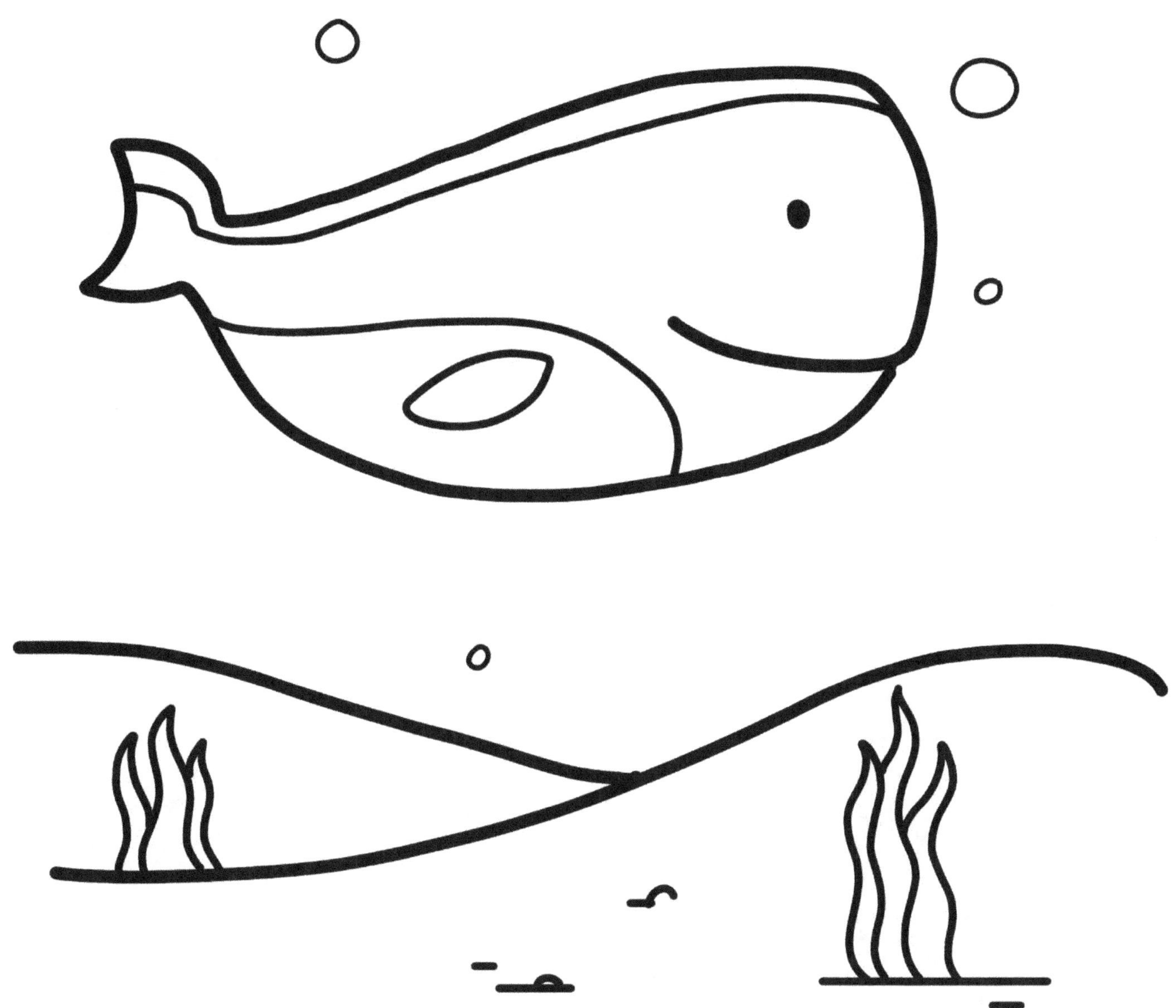